One World

On the Move

Valerie Guin

W

FRANKLIN WATTS
LONDON • SYDNEY

Note
about the series
One World is designed
to encourage young
readers to find out more
about people and places
in the wider world. The
photographs have been
carefully selected to
stimulate discussion
and comparison.

First published in 2004 by Franklin Watts
96 Leonard Street, London EC2A 4XD

Franklin Watts Australia
45-51 Huntley Street, Alexandria, NSW 2015

© Franklin Watts 2004

Editor: Caryn Jenner
Designer: Louise Best
Art director: Jonathan Hair
Maps: Ian Thompson
Reading consultant: Hilary Minns, Institute of Education, Warwick University

Acknowledgements: Adrian Arbib/Still Pictures: 12. Bob Battersby/Eye Ubiquitous: 23b.
Nigel Cattlin/Holt Studios: 6. James Davis Worldwide: 16b,18t, 22, 23t. Bennett Dean/Eye
Ubiquitous: 21. Mark Edwards/Still Pictures: 17. Robert Francis/Hutchison: 16t. Angela
Hampton/Ecoscene: 10. Jeremy Horner/Hutchison: 8. Luc Hosten/ Ecoscene: 19. Oldrich
Karasek/Still Pictures: 11. Robert Landau/Corbis: 9. Ray Moller: 7. NASA: 27. NASA/Eye
Ubiquitous: 26. Edward Parker/Hutchison: 14. Joe Pasieka/Eye Ubiquitous: 13t. Christine
Pemberton/Hutchison: 13b. Harmut Schwarzbach/Still Pictures: 15. Paul Thompson/Eye
Ubiquitous: 24. Isabella Tree/Hutchison: endpapers, 2, 3, 25. Nick Wildman/Eye
Ubiquitous: 18b. Michael S. Yamashita/Corbis: 20.

A CIP catalogue record for this book is available from the British Library

ISBN 0 7496 5438 4

Printed in Malaysia

Contents

Getting about

People all around the world
need to **travel** from one place
to another. They use many
ways of getting about.

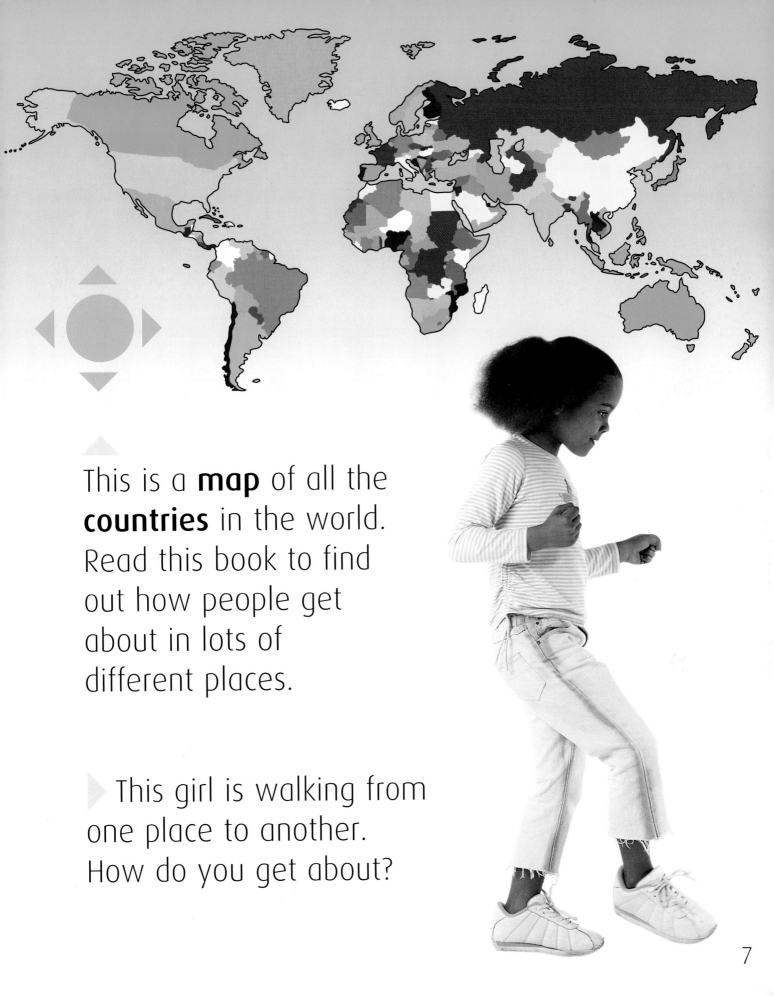

This is a **map** of all the **countries** in the world. Read this book to find out how people get about in lots of different places.

▶ This girl is walking from one place to another. How do you get about?

Cars

In some places, cars fill the roads. This traffic jam is in the **city** of Bangkok in Thailand. There are more than 2 million cars in Bangkok.

In the **countryside**, where fewer people live, there are fewer cars. This road is in Italy.

Bicycles

People often ride bikes for fun. These children are cycling on a special bike path in the United States.

In many countries, people cycle to work. These people are riding their bikes to work in Chengdu, a city in China.

Riding animals

In Mongolia, people ride horses to get about. Families often own a whole herd of horses, and children learn to ride when they are very young.

In the desert of Sudan, people often ride camels. A camel can travel a long way across the dry desert without needing a drink.

Most elephants in Nepal are wild. But some elephants are trained to carry people and **goods**.

13

Boats

These people in Peru live in small **villages** around a lake. They use a boat to travel about. The man at the front pushes the boat through the water with a long pole.

People can take their cars across the water on this ferry boat in Kenya. The ferry ride is much shorter than driving all the way around by road.

Buses and trams

▶ People in Panama can get about on colourful buses called "chivas".

◀ In Britain, people ride on double decker buses. Passengers climb the stairs inside the bus to get to the top floor.

In cities like Amsterdam in the Netherlands, people can take trams to get about. Trams run on tracks through the streets.

Trains

This bullet train zooms past Mount Fuji in Japan. The bullet train is one of the fastest trains in the world.

Underground trains are a quick way to get about in cities. This one runs in Moscow in Russia.

This steam train in South Africa carries tourists across the steep hills and valleys so they can see the beautiful countryside.

Delivering things

These boats are carrying bricks
down the Grand Canal in China.
The Grand Canal is a man-made
river. Boats use the canal to carry
goods from place to place.

This road train carries goods for large **distances** across Australia. The driver sits in the truck at the front, which pulls the trailers along the long empty roads – like a train without tracks.

Going for a ride

▶ Instead of roads, the city of Venice in Italy has canals filled with water. People ride about the city in boats called gondolas.

In the city of Rio de Janeiro in Brazil, people can take a cable car up to the top of Sugar Loaf Mountain.

During the snowy winters in Norway, people can go for a ride in a dog sled.

In the air

An aeroplane flies powerfully through the sky. It can carry people for long distances very fast. This aeroplane has just taken off from an airport in Spain.

A hot-air balloon drifts slowly through the sky. The passengers in this hot-air balloon in Namibia are looking for wild animals.

In space

It's lift off! Rockets fire the space shuttle up into the sky. The rockets give the shuttle extra power to fly out to space, then they drop away.

In space, astronauts travel
high above the Earth in the
space shuttle orbiter.

All around the world

All over the world, people use many ways to get about.

United States

Brazil

Panama

Peru

The countries that you have read about are shown in pink on this map of the world. Find the country that matches each picture in the book.

Britain

Netherlands

Norway

Russia   Mongolia

Japan

China

Italy

Nepal

Spain

Sudan   Thailand

Kenya

Australia

South Africa

Namibia

Glossary

city a large town where lots of people live and work

countries places with their own governments

countryside land that is natural without many houses

distances the space between places

goods things that are bought and sold

map a drawing that shows where places are located

travel to move from one place to another

villages small towns, usually in the countryside

Index

30